Where Silence Gets Loud:

Poems on Introspection, Acceptance, and Letting Go

by Olga Gabris

Where Silence Gets Loud:
Poems on Introspection, Acceptance, and Letting Go

Published by: Coffee Cup Productions
Cover and Interior Art: Victor Tricerri

ISBN print: 979-8-9963853-0-0
ISBN ebook: 979-8-9963853-3-1

Published in the United States of America.

First edition, 2026

This is a work of creative expression. Any resemblance to actual persons, living or deceased, or actual events is coincidental unless otherwise indicated.

With any inquiries, please contact
olga@coffeecupproductions.com

Dedication

To all the survivors –
You know who you are.

Table of Contents

Foreword

The entertainment industry – whether film, literature, or music – is filled with expectations that often pull artists away from themselves. This collection of poems became my attempt to challenge that machinery and return to something more honest.

Publishing these pieces feels vulnerable. Visibility can often resemble exposure, and the process itself can become overwhelming. But those moments pass. This book is a reminder that turbulence, no matter how consuming it feels, is temporary.

Telling stories has always been both my means of survival and my reason to continue. I hope that somewhere within these pages, you find a reason to continue, as well.

~Olga

Encapsulated Loneliness

Every tiny note

Or, more precisely,
A lack of,
Is comparable to a cut,
A bruise,
A pain
Which can leave or can stay...
An unanswered email
Or missed call
Can often leave scars
Or burn marks.
Each question with no answer
Is its own dilemma,
A cliff-hanger,
A well with no exit,
It only gets deeper.
Some of them heal,
And some – become dormant.
Each shared link
Longs to be opened,
Each statement,
Or comment
Is a mini-love letter
Still waiting,
So dearly,
To find its purpose.

six feet... above –
see you there.
this could be love
or despair.
what is the name
but a packaging?
playing the game
of the savages.

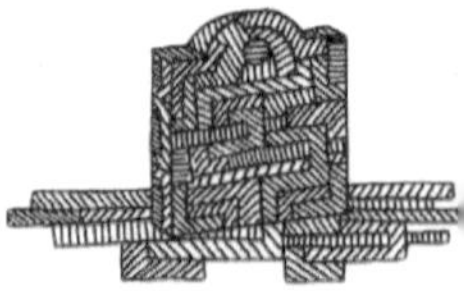

I never believed in perfection,
denying its beauty and grace.
avoiding my own reflection,
I hid and averted my gaze.
While others came out of closets
and added that sparkle and gloss,
I battled the ones who are close,
forgetting the sentence of loss.
They said, "It's ok, you can join us,
you're strange but it isn't your fault".
Acceptance was never my purpose –
I've taken it, dusted with salt.
I tried to believe in relation
of intellect, mind and soul,
to only uncover damnation,
where everyone's playing a role.
They faked to adore me, to only
achieve their goals and leave.
I've learned to ignore all the lonely,
when lonely and broken is me.
If nothing remains authentic,
why should I? – Most likely, because
when world's overrun with synthetics,
I'll find someone truly close.

I want
clarity,
honesty,
is that too much?
I thought we agreed
on importance
of trust,
communication,
respect,
openness,
fair expression...
Maybe a mild depression,
or something greater,
to come.
What have I done?
Where have you gone?
Neural sandpaper
is my preferred cocoon.
give me a spoon –
soon,
we can share this sorbet.
I am a tiny bit morbid,
doing this mental ballet.
So, your suggestion
is density,
gravity,

common sense –
wonderful,
call me when done.
I'm hearing the void –
it's a pleasant narrator.
It means something greater,
it doesn't avoid.
It accepts.
Have you overslept?
I'm reading your visions.
Incision
to memories,
thoughts,
and illusions...
Your quiet conclusion
of theories
I never forgot.

Long term

Long distance
Lukewarm
Good riddance
Though, is it?
This hole
Swallowing
Not teasing
Not easy
Nothing, really
Lonely
Alone
All gone
But memories...
Small victories,
Big fall...

burning through the fabric of reality,
scraping the insides of tired brain,
pushing boundaries of standardized normality,
moving onto alien terrain;
breaking laws of someone else's reason,
asking questions to the universe and self;
faking adaptation to new season,
being half-expired, not expelled;
making choices to somehow keep on going,
taking chances to survive and then – to live,
learning is not better than not knowing,
giving orders when it's time to give,
getting to the point: there, far away,
will be left an old as world motif:
when the night becomes your greatest day,
in the end, you ask yourself: What if?

Black patches on the moon,
Wholeheartedly
I'm viewing in monsoon,
Repeatedly.
For every crater-scar,
Astonishing
A name of a rock star,
Half-vanishing.
It's hidden in plain sight,
Remarkably.
Whenever someone died,
A traveler
Picked up their remains,
Delivered.
There is no angel-saint
Artillery.
They travel at midnight,
Encompassing
Escape of every life,
All surfaces.
They scout and inspect
The liveliness
Of humans and insects:
No boundaries.
There is no certain date,
No promises;

I'd love to terminate
This loneliness.
They tell me, it's alright:
The calendar
Will set the date and time
For everyone.

For happiness,
you travel so far,
beyond imagination,
premonition,
neglecting fears
and existing pre-condition,
adapting everything for this translation,
so common sense does not exist or matter,
composing life as if it were a letter,
the travel can and will repair scars,
to light your path under the starry sky –
so fast, and then – a heartbeat – slow,
through winds and heavy northern snow,
and none of that will matter or apply,
when you decide to live your life,
not just survive,
you'll always find your way among the darkness.

It's his birthday again –
Man I love, unconditionally.
Not romantically, not sustainably,
By decision.
I love him for living.
For seeing
The world from all angles,
Fighting demons,
But more frequently – angels.
Just for being
And breathing the atmosphere
Shared with all,
And not really here.

—

There are people who come
To support us,
Others teach us, or can
Leave impromptu.
Some would love us,
Not always mutual,
Others cross the path
Like a vulture.
There are people also
With an aura
That transcends it all,
Opens doors.

So soon,
11 will be 12 –
Full moon
Is looking at the city,
Its light can't help
The loneliness,
Its overwhelming pity
Of regret.
Such emptiness
Is filling to the brim
You can't forget.
The shadows
Are cast.
They stretch the skies,
Creating poetry of night:
Forgotten past,
The gallows,
The sorrow in your eyes
You can't deny.
So, go on:
Disrupt the night.
Stand up and fill
Your heart with thoughts
That hurt the most.
You have to carry on.
And all's alright.
Remember: not a thing
Is better than you've got –
Until it's lost.

Your eyes are made of molten metal,
The darkest, deepest shade of black.
I can't recall – have we met, yet?
If not, I want to go back
And make it happen. Only then,
This life will get much more compelling.
It doesn't matter where or when,
Let the timeline do storytelling.

—

There's something comforting in broken glass;
its texture, for instance, is remarkable:
it can't become the whole piece again,
and yet, the imperfection makes it palpable.
It cannot claim the vanity of gloss,
nor can it win the best of the awards –
and yet, for someone *something* that is lost
is worth so much until the point it hurts.

with all these paragraphs, it's hard to choose a title,
among the stream of information in my head.
there's so much more my memory is hiding –
these thoughts will only stop when I'm dead.
while trying to avoid the real calling,
creating something for someone and not myself,
I didn't think this life was so lonely,
and I don't want this loneliness to dwell.
to break the barriers, I must continue writing,
creating, making things with no regret.
this is my way of modern, peaceful fighting,
which makes me more alive, before I'm dead.

Something is missing:
perception of home.
It was never easy,
aimless I roam.
Accepting rejection,
still quite eager.
I'm missing connection,
you long for more freedom.

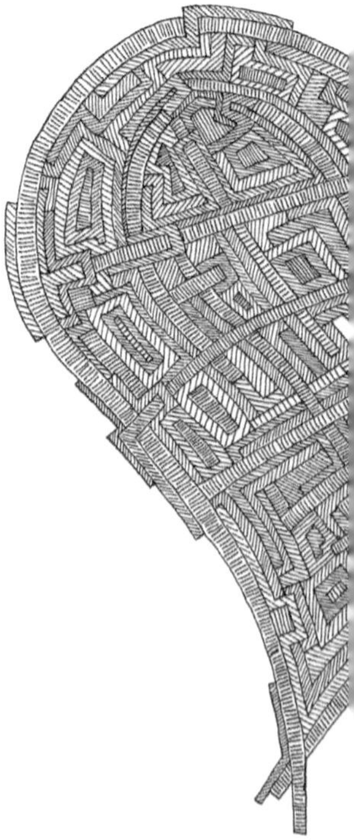

are you sorry for the times
I was sorry for,
talking quietly;
sorry for the sad smiles
you have seen before
almost nightly;
saddened by the pain
of the days
we won't live again...
was it all in vain?
cannot comprehend,
washed away by rain.
I could never breathe
with you sad,
feeling bothered;
never found peace –
only grief,
feeling smothered.
are you happy then,
with me gone,
feeling limitless?
I do wish you well,
need to run,
time is priceless.

Tell me some-thing.
Not any-thing,
but words of wit and wisdom;
"To thy beloved kingdom,
I bring my heart,
and let you be the king."
It may be a good start
if you forget to think –
and lose yourself, within.

Your dressing table
told me more
of your day
than you did;
it enabled
half-forgotten
transcript.
Armoire-memories,
to the core,
they will stay
and continue
expanding.
Last man standing,
or a woman,
someone true,
with a lineage.

All-black everything,
black coffee,
darker life outlook
don’t mean that something
is missing,
don’t equal lonely;
this pattern can be completed
with some dark chocolate
and a book.

Du spinnst (German for "you're crazy")

My head is spinning –
So blurry now.
I'm in denial.
This new new ordeal
Is not ideal,
You can't escape
This new beginning.
Still processing –
I'm thirsty.
My soul's empty.
When you return –
No one is winning.
The pace of space
Is violent.
Your eyes are violet.
I've never seen
Such everything
Behind the scenes.
In your embrace,
So prominent.
"Have a nice life"
Is not a lie,
It's f*cking fabulous.
Or maybe, scandalous.

I spin the net
Of what-if-stories,
With morbid glory.
I spin, du *spinnst.*
How marvelous.

I scratch you off.
I tear my thoughts,
My head,
My memories,
My heart.
It's just too much.
It's all been said.
We never go back.
It's not that hard.
It's not too bad.
I don't regret.
We cannot stay
Like this.
Move on.
Forgive, forget.
And never recollect.

Chaotic Times

Creating a pattern
of randomness,
slicing the strata
of wholeness,
letting it shatter –
awkwardness
has all your data
and memories.

Solace

The problem is,
I feel too much.
It's not my wish –
I can't control it.
This life
is closing down on me,
I let it, but I never want it.
The noises.
in and outside my head
consume the silence,
poison peace.
What if tomorrow – I'm dead,
where will it be,
my final solace?
I struggle with myself,
the world
just keeps on running,
always will be.
It's not the emptiness,
per se,
it's this amazing, stunning
Freedom.

Unrequested,
unrequited,
those dreams
never quieted.
Never tamed
or co-sensored,
in the name
of my common sense.
Walking blindly,
undecided,
was it mutual,
or one-sided?
Quite angular
and peculiar
dreams are modular –
twisted, truly.

The ones and zeros can't capture all the essence,
They can't describe condition of your heart:
This subtle, soft, majestic effervescence
Of fragile matter, yet to become a form of art –
To come alive, and breathe, and move the feelings
Of those who can live and be alive.
It's frankly, difficult, among us human beings,
To find those who can do more than just survive.
We're buried in this dynamic clutter,
Too busy to step out of the scheme.
All the devices cannot help us being smarter,
Without turning into someone's living memes.
An artist has to burn, destroying minds,
While painting real, not just prettiest of things.
We only have this life, so make it count,
The beauty's found where the questioning begins.

Why don't you kill me
quite literally,
openly,
finally;
why not remove
obliteration
of dying
mentally,
virtually,
philosophically...
It's tiring
emotionally
to be waiting,
hoping,
longing,
procrastinating,
creating
a sense
of belonging
where none
is attainable
or rather,
sustainable.
If dying
is lesser in time
or in effort,

I'd rather decline
other offer
to be in suspension
in this dimension
of hope
to where there is none.
So let it be gone,
really,
blissfully,
honestly,
willingly...
with no one.

Composing passwords of forgotten circumstances;
Combining memories into a story for tomorrow.
I know, soon, there will be no more of second chances,
No more regrets from others I could borrow.

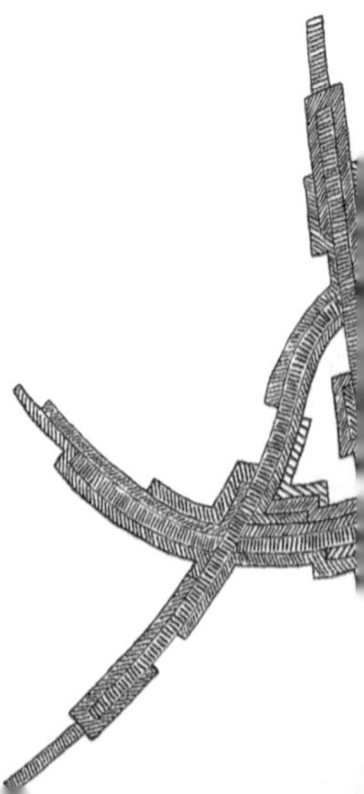

To un-contaminate
The mindset,
One cannot ever hibernate
Or choose preset.
By forging paths to take
and lives to live,
One puts the self at stake
to get and give.

scarred fingers,
a small burn,
a paper cut?
what the hell happened?
a phone call,
wait – no more,
I'll check email,
unbothered.
oh, but
notifications
flood all my screen,
DMs.
requests.
and invitations –
forgot to mention:
I'm tired of them.
someone is texting.
another junk
in my inbox.
and letterbox.
and at the parking.
again, distracted.
my finger hurts.
how did I –
wait, no time.
I have to run.
but there's traffic,
so problematic.
the sun
is blinding,
I need to travel more.

eat healthier.
sleep better.
oh, but the weather
is not too bad,
there is a sale
at the bookstore,
apparently.
I want some tea.
do I have gas?
ok, it's drivable.
I need to eat.
how are my plants?
forgot to water them,
the finger hurts.
the outskirts
and the suburbs
are cheaper.
I'm not a cheater.
just lost a bit.
the light is lit.
another text –
I'll read at home.
it looks enormous!
the rain starts falling.
I'll sleep till morning.
it's dark again,
another day.
another pile of letters
and emails.
I need to shower.
the end.

Sleep is an elusive beast

It's so completely mystical,
Got out of my system,
Cannot resist it.
I'm trying, but it's just too much –
I'm out of touch.
Reality is something I don't know;
Will there be another show?
And even now I'm deciding
In which direction I am gliding.
So hard to keep on track
The time is gone, can't go back.
So much to do, important things –
Instead, I'm here, writing nonsense.
Or, is it? It's subjective.
I've gotten so good deflecting
My day by day, the bigger picture
Sometimes, don't notice the adventure.
There's so much to write, to think
I'm so in, forget to blink.
Small pieces of reactions, daily thoughts?
Someone I've met, someone – have not.
The problem is, I cannot chill.
Your living normal – no thrill.
What's normal? A complete illusion.
I'm tired of my own confusion.
Too many plans, too many thoughts
Not all of them depend on me, of what

I can complete.
And many others – obsolete
Because I cannot find synergy
Or energy; eternal blasphemy
Of things I can't deliver;
All I can do is keep on living.
There are some days where I don't want to,
But moving forward is my motto.

No substance is enough to make me stop.
I will keep going until the day I drop.
Not breaking any laws, not bending rules –
I won't succumb to ordinance of mules.

To every chaos, there is a proper answer.
Too bad too few control the circumstances.
I'd better die still questioning the norm,
Than live, regretting making choices to conform.

It's not the first time

I feel my veins being pulled,
Twisted and turned into knots –
Truly, is this all you've got?
I still believe my glass is half full.
Trying to break me – go on,
Crush all my bones, like dreams.
If it's too much, as it seems –
Worry not. I want to be strong.
Losing hope is worse than the pain.
You can drain me, but I will survive.
Getting stronger with every new dive,
I'm refilling my glass, yet again.
...Should I recover, can't decide...
If all my scars – on the inside...

Self-proclaimed critical stage
Doesn't always result in crisis,
When the emphasis is
On the average.

———

Here's "low end" of the low,
A heartbeat alarmingly slow,
Where we don't feel any pleasure
Numbness is our new treasure.

Racing
on razor
my thoughts
and ideas,
cannot deny
the absence of sleep.
Paving
the grave
for could-nots
and un-reals,
until I die
I will smile
and not weep.

you have to drop it –
far and deep,
beyond the line,
above horizon.
your quite wobbly,
flat and weak,
suppressed, sublime,
unwanted pardon.

Nihilistic Tendencies

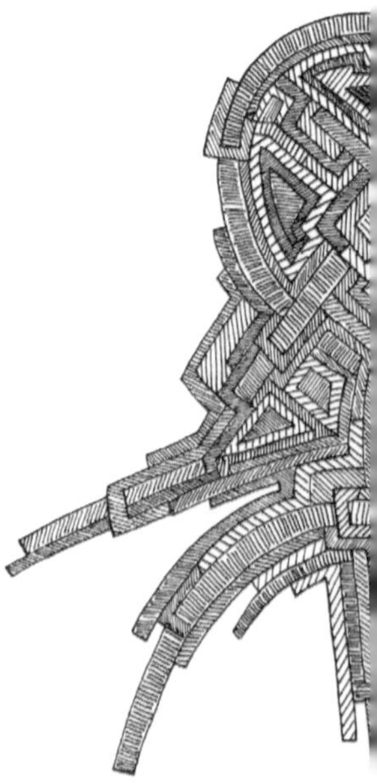

The inside of your eyelids
Can be very colorful,
Or dark, depending on what you believe in.
There could be smiles
Of angels and gods
Or demons, depending on what you believe in.
There may be waves
Of emotions – in ranges,
From lows to highs, depending on how you love.
You find meaning,
And purpose, and truth
In measures, proportional to the depth of your love.

The second chances

Religion promises
Are acts of violence
On common sense.
Don't need eternity
To contemplate,
The future's earned
Day after day.

A dotted line is not enough –
Its boundaries are weak and factual.
This choice of yours has made me laugh –
Your last goodbye is way too casual.
I see you hanging; silent, thoughtful –
Why would you choose to leave this life?
Can't help it – I'm not feeling awful,
For where you fell, I will survive.
Too little time for all these questions,
You left it all for me to solve.
I'm done – not aiming for perfection,
What's left for me, I'll live it all.

I do not fancy
the literacy
In self-expression.
All the raw edges
Hug best.

Ice
breath
life
death
kiss
kill
miss
me
cut
deep
shut
sleep.

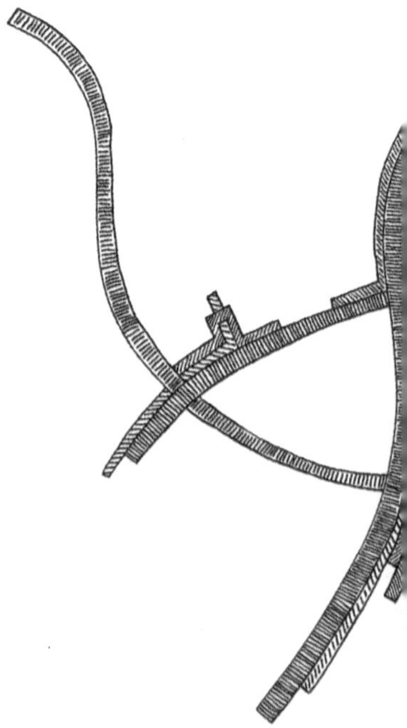

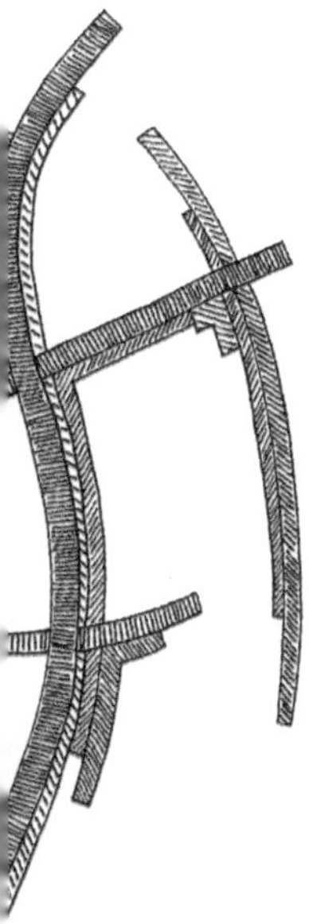

spectacular spectrum
reflecting on scleras
inviting illusion
of all things to come,
deflecting the vector
of big atmospheric
galactic confusion
this life has become.

---

a plastic reaction
to someone's refraction
creates disillusion
in matters of life.
with true satisfaction
by pushing to action,
you make the conclusion
to live and to fight.

Lifting up, piece by piece,
All these fragments of my soul.
Was it ever up to me,
Or perhaps, all predetermined?
Preselected and preset,
By default, hard-coded, standard...
Even if it was, I can't
Live my life with such a bargain.
No matter how it spins,
I decide what's next in line.
Let them count all my sins –
Common sense cannot decline
All the rational suggestions;
In the end, I'll pay in full.
Every single recollection
Evens out at a null.
I stand up for all my actions,
Own my mistakes and faults,
So in the end, audacious,
I won't switch to the default.

On the steep cliff under the darkest sky,
Wisest trees crowned over unknown kind:
Haunting winds' whispers went wild,
Inviting to this world a new kind of child.
Its skin pale, eyes – ghostly white,
Long, wispy hair made of darkest midnight,
Lips – so red, craving for blood,
All forest creatures welcome a new god.
Leader of Earth, nemesis of men,
Bringing to justice offenders of land.
Striking his final, defining accord:
Hail, Earthlings, to the planet's new lord.

There will be no more
of quiet tolling.
The ringer's dead,
and bell is long forgotten.
What's left is loneliness,
it's bigger than the sun,
and almost brighter too,
since nothing's left to lighten.

Cutting –
I can understand its beauty,
Stunning pattern.
Someone's call of duty,
Someone's pain...
Everything depends on the objective.
Deeper, as we merge into collective
Till the moment last internal dragon slain.
We proceed, and feel no regret.
Let the red replace this creamy satin.
A guarantee the goals are met:
Cutting.

It's staring back at me, suspended.
I freeze, not sure how to proceed.
Distracted, I can't help but feel offended –
The moment's lost; I can't regain my speed.
The thoughts, the memories, ideas, aspirations –
Again are buried somewhere deep inside.
If I believed in afterlife, then my damnation
Would be this endless roller coaster ride.
I'd feel alive, inspired and awaken,
Then gather all my tools and writing props,
To try and prove this theory mistaken –
Yet staring at blank canvas never stops.

On the edge of universe,
Hidden from the common sight,
There is sunlight in reverse,
Dusk in place of day and night.
Winds caress the endless deserts,
Trees so tall – they touch the sky.
Will we ever learn the lesson
And, instead of dreaming, try?
Go forth without looking,
Run ahead, so wild and free.
So much freedom sounds spooky –
Most of them do not agree.
Yet, until the days are over,
We must challenge the routine.
There is no greater sorrow
Than observing common scene.

Neglecting the complexity of patterns,
Forgetting the mechanics of the trade,
You carry on the wisdom's shining lantern,
No matter how many changes have been made.
Reality is brutal, unforgiving,
And yet – inspiring, honest, kind, picturesque.
You still enjoy the magic of the living
With all its beauty and its wonderful grotesque.

I've never left –
the empty feeling
has manifested from the void.
Alive or dead,
above the ceiling,
I hang with feelings un-deployed.

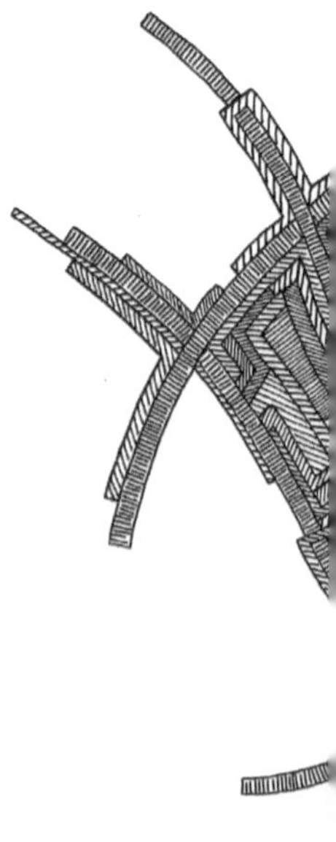

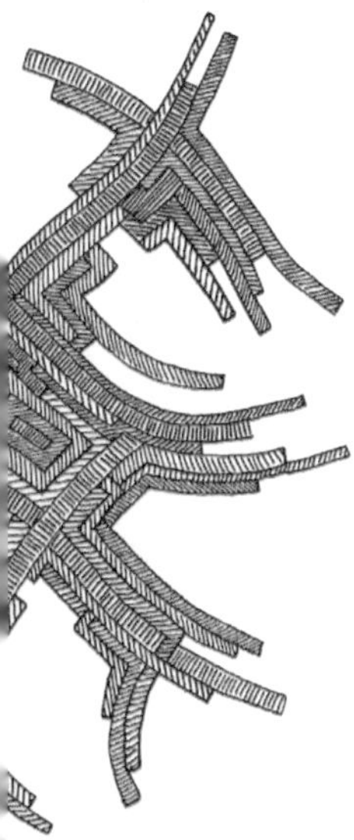

The standard set is no longer standard,
The puzzle's getting more complex by day.
If there's only one, most brutal tyrant –
Then it's your memory, with all its cruel sway.
Reopening the scars of times forgotten,
Replacing brief excitement with despair,
Was there ever quality or quota
Of what was damaged then, beyond repair?
It's ripping conscience to shreds, to pieces,
And leaving you with emptiness inside.
Once path is burnt, there will be no easy
Way. Get hurt and learn, repeat, and fight.
Fight for yourself, the real you.
When world is filled with copies of templates,
It will be left with tiniest of crews:
The ones who stayed away from duplicates.

While juggling words,
and thoughts,
and calendars,
We bring the swords
of poets
to the altars.
They shine through darkness,
shameless,
naked with the truth –
will fight the blindness
of masses:
Verse vermouth.

Silence
is on the other side of clarity;
on the edge,
hovering
at the brink of utter-reality,
lingering
over knowledge.
Violence
cannot ever bring purpose,
or else –
it's not mindful;
simmering
with the reason
for safety.

It's sunset-time, I'm running through the grass.
The sun is warm and gentle; so forgiving.
Do you remember years that have passed?
For me, the memories sometimes replace the living.

So beautiful and peaceful, I'm in awe –
Tonight replaced the myriads of lonely evenings.
I'll never leave behind what I saw,
While savoring this promising beginning.

Final Escape

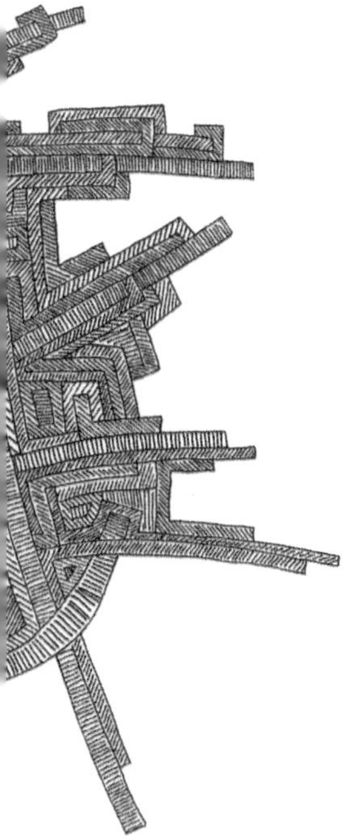

All dreaming, wondering,
fulfilling, giving,
exploring, pondering,
embracing, living,
imagining
and gentle-caring
courageous
life-better-sharing...

Don't worry, my darling –
You'll be fine.
You will survive and what's better:
You thrive
Through the weather.
It can be unsettling, at times.
It wears you out, and dries
Remaining regrets and retries.
That's why, you will have to
Survive.
I know you can,
As do you.
Together, we went till curfew.
I won't be alone, over there.
You go with me, everywhere.
I see you, and feel you,
We won't be apart –
It's only a different start.
This life could have never deceived you.
There is only one redirection:
I am in another dimension.
I saw your magnificent wings
Through the winds,
Your careful, beautiful flying,
The faster was only me dying.
They took me away so quickly.
My body felt almost liquid.

Observing the skies,
Not hearing the cries
Of the living,
I'm tired of lies,
I cut all my ties –
Please forgive me.
They rolled up my sheets
And folded my feet
In the coffin.
I never signed up for the morphine...
Don't tell me you want otherwise:
Keep going, you will survive.

When breathing itself is a torture,
We just want to avoid all this pain,
Desire some comfort and closure,
Seeking unbridled terrain.
Wounds of others become obsolete,
Who wants more than already in sight?
We deflect, overcome and compete
In this endless and merciless fight.
Fight for living. For being alive.
But for what? A rhetorical question.
So busy – we want to survive,
Still forgetting the imminent lecture
Of this world. Of being a person.
Basic truths of this mortal archive.
While attempting to reach the next version,
We forget how to live, then we die.

Pouring midnight
on top of
reality;
sending signal
to stop
immortality,
I began fantasize
of an alternate
life,
no lie,
overdrive,
all forgotten,
deprived,
to survive
and still thrive,
loving life,
losing time,
never-minding
mortal decline,
and still counting
from the bottom.

The quiet whisper
Is full of wisdom,
While sharing knowledge
Of the past.
I am a listener
Of all this whistling;
Dark heritage
That didn't last.

I always dreamt of Otherlife –
Alternative, with hidden meaning.
With no drama, no lies,
Ideal, like a movie screening.
I tried to build it on this earth,
Repairing broken and dismantled –
Despair was my final earn,
Unable to sustain this cradle.
I searched as high as summer sky,
As low, as deep winter's midnight.
Yet, no one could hear me cry –
There's no father, only children.

The night is closing in, I feel its breath.
It wisps like many winds, it howls like wolves.
The color of the sky has reached its depth,
Can’t take my eyes away – I’m so involved.
So close – I can sense it on my skin.
Its touch is cool and gentle, like moonlight.
I’m here for a reason, to begin
Embracing darkness, welcoming the night.
My name is called, there's no turning back.
I close my eyes, get ready for impact.
If only I survive this night’s attack,
I’ll know everything there is in living act.

Again, a drop of yesterday
is drying out on the surface.
It's gone, as it can never stay
Beyond its brief deliverance.
Of course, tomorrow will come
with only what's in store for then;
it's beating quiet, steady drum
which only lasts a day, and when
again, a new duration of this life,
a smaller subset of forever
will start its own course and die
remaining punctual and clever.

Last Wish

Perhaps, I spoke too soon.
All my requests about death
Exploded, like a thin balloon,
Forgetting to enjoy each breath –
I wanted it to stop. The breathing,
I thought, I've had enough to live.
Somehow, death was only teasing
It can take life, but cannot give.
Besides, I never wanted strangers
To talk about me and cry.
There are so many real dangers
In life, and that you can't deny.
I wanted to become unknown
And disappear into smoke.
So no one would see the show,
But... life has brought a cruel joke
And now, you're gone instead.
I can't believe this is the end.
How did it happen – you're dead,
And I still have some time to spend?
You didn't tell me your last wish,
So now I will never know.
I'm glad you had some time with me,
And we will catch another show.

Later

They say the death is quite lonely,
And nothing's truly what it seems.
However, I enjoy this journey,
Not sure wholly, what that means.
I now know: time's the answer
To all the questions of mankind.
Life doesn't offer second chances –
Don't let emotions make you blind.
Day after day, we are suspended
In time, and space, and in between.
So, while you live – enough pretending,
Let people see what you have seen.

Her thoughts are on my mind; her devotion –
I live it every day, in slow motion.
She shows me the way, but I don't follow:
She is inside me, meaning, I'm not hollow.

—

I'm drawing a pattern, it's a tricky one:
So many shapes stem from this pool of red.
You'll see the final version when it's done,
I won't be breathing, if it truly is the end.

—

I received your final goodbye:
tooth for a tooth, and eye for an eye.
Were you about to take me with?
I won't be joining, but will give you a kiss.

we rise in silence,
we ride in silence.
to low horizon,
toward the darkness.

before the sunrise,
below the stars,
along the riverside,
across the mountains.

we leave at midnight,
then march till dawn,
to pave the overpass,
until it's gone.

we see a morning light,
then face the dusk,
there is no better ride,
no one to ask.

no one to say it's right,
or prove it wrong,
until the exit sign,
we ride alone...

Your fingers froze, as is half-sentence
While typing out state of heart:
The sad and stunning reminiscence
Of times before we were apart.
This slow motion, tough decision:
To go forth, or reconsider?
Then – quick and thorough incision,
You're ready to move on; so eager.
It's dripping red, creating patterns –
The images of afterlife.
Is it dark there? I'll bring a lantern
To light the path: both yours and mine.
You're still; I'm still around – lately,
There is no better place to be.
We lived this life, enjoying greatly
All things that killed both you and me.

no ambitions,
sorrows,
or renditions.
just not this moment
of torment,
the glimmer of truth...
about you,
for tomorrow.

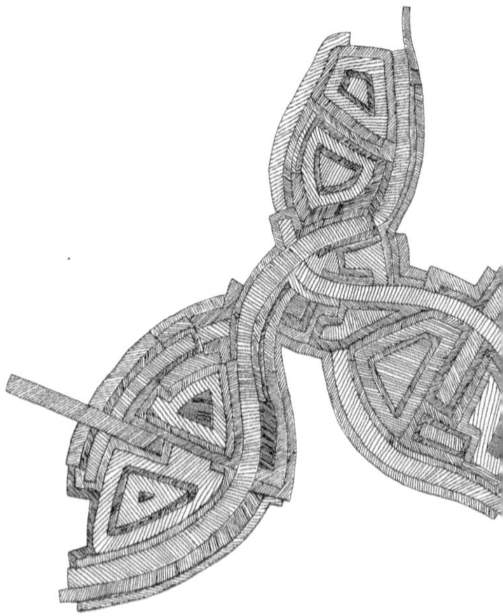

Don’t want to live

Don’t want to live,
Don’t want to die.
So sick
Of this so-called life.
Confused,
Abused
For the sake of the
Amused.

No, I don’t really want to die,
I’m just done being alive.
I’m tired of this violence
Someone calls obedience.

I’m done.
Don’t want to have this life.
Don’t want to take my life.
Someone?

I close my eyes
To see the blackness,
To feel the madness
Don’t want this life.
Alive.
Am I?

I feel no pain –
Dead nerves, dead veins.
Exhausted,
Exposed,
Out in the open,
Cut up and broken.
Don't want to live,
Don't want to die.
So sick
Of this so-called life.

Suicidal

When they text you,
"I'm in the tub" –
You don't imagine relaxing
Under warm, fuzzy bubbles,
You ask if they're ok.
Because "in the tub" can mean
Many things.
And it's not even that common,
It's what the media wants us to think.
We romanticize dying by cutting
Somewhere warm and forgiving.
When they say they're fine
But their eye is twitching,
And you're catching that
Because no one can,
Because you know what it's like.
And you pretend, and comply with the lie
That everything is really fine,
But maybe, could be tolerable,
Not as painful.
So you nod, and agree,
And let them see through you:
I'm here, I *get* you.
Because not feeling seen
Is worse than being alone.
"Alone" is not loneliness,
It's peace. The loneliness

Is when sadness really hits.
Yes, you have your devices
And tools – all the usuals.
Keep moving, get busy,
Distract by the visuals.
When someone else is smiley,
But there's a void in their eyes
You don't ask, "What's wrong?"
You say, "I'm here, if you need me".
You never ask someone critical
Why they want to end their life.
It's the most cruel question there is.
Everyone has their reasons –
We don't always see them.
It's a blessing to never experience
That gentle pull to delirium
With so many options around.
It's the absence of sound.
It just is.
It can change.
But usually, it's built-in
Like a factory setting.
And you learn how to live
All your life,
Always knowing, rarely aware
Not willing to welcome despair –
But when someone does,
You admit it:
It's better than feeling guilty.

It’s a personal choice.
It’s a way of life, a philosophy.
With all its delight and monstrosity.
So when someone says,
“You’re killing it!”
You think to yourself,
Better "it", than myself,
And keep living.

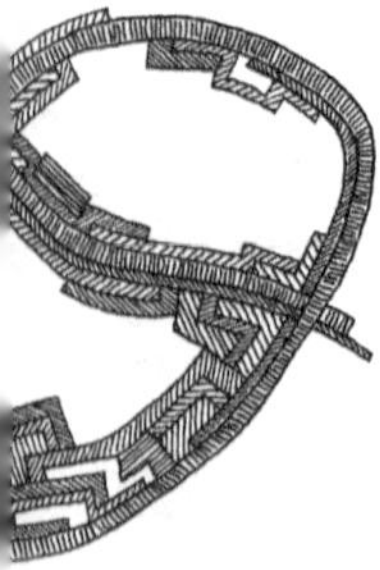

Acknowledgements

To everyone who chose this book: even if you only read fragments of it, something may have spoken to you. I hope it continues speaking to others, too.

Oksana Homutinni: your eyes, mind, and *essence* amaze me. Thank you for being my closest friend and trusted ally for nearly two decades.

Helena Fowler: how someone can be this intelligent and mindful continues to inspire me. Thank you for leading by example.

To the beta-readers, who kept it honest and offered invaluable insights: Ariel Aviad, Aaron Maleare, Sid Sikder, Daniel T.

To the VNF core team: Unni Rav, your no-BS-but-with-a-heart approach is next level. KD Karnati, you know we can always make the sequel more graphic.

To Victor Tricerri, for your art and your kindness.

Tony Gapastione: your ability to keep going is a brand. Please package and offer it at a premium.

Other friends, colleagues, and beautiful humans: you're all stars now, in this... *live* show!

JP Gendelmeyer, Daniel Knop, Keith Churchill, Mario Vaerewijck, Ron Graves, Ron Edwards, Nick Nimick, Tal Shrey, Michael Clay, Angela Yesson, Philippe Blache, Jon Villegas, Ryan Molyneaux, Lisa-Maria Tertsus, Scott Sommers, Quinn Vitakis, Gabriel Bocanegra, Shraddha Sansare Upadhye, Billy Finnegan, Kriti Singh, Esha Shah, Richa Singhal, Raymond Lin, Amanda Daniels, Mary Holden – thank you.

Simon Rahm (Jesus on Extasy): few people see the world through such a similar lens. The future will set the *score*.

Johan Van Roy (Suicide Commando)... An entirely separate book would not be enough to describe the impact you've had on this world, and on me personally. Thank you for being born.

And to anyone unintentionally omitted: you were still part of the story.

About the Artist

Born in La Spezia, Italy in the early 1970s, Victor studied liberal arts, philosophy, and the classics before pursuing his scientific curiosity through aerospace engineering, earning a master's degree from the University of Pisa.

At the beginning of the new millennium, he relocated to San Francisco, where he currently lives and creates.

Art remains Victor's deepest passion, expressed through poetry, illustration, and painting. His work exists at the intersection of geometry and abstraction. Core themes include curves arranged into paths and imagined landscapes, as well as spaces filled with both darkness and light. This unique shifting perspective reveals his deeply personal interpretation of the surrounding world.

Scan QR code to learn more, or visit
https://www.vaictor.com/

About the Author

Olga Gabris is a writer, film director, producer, poet, and gothic minimalist based in the San Francisco Bay. She describes her personal brand as "Morbid Optimist" as a nod to her dark, yet hopeful, narratives. In her work, Olga explores the intricacies of the human psyche and forces behind people's actions.

Olga is the founder of Coffee Cup Productions, a multimedia production company with a focus on mental health, emotional well-being, and intellectual resilience. Her other passions include learning new languages, interior design, and getting lost in graveyards with a cup of black coffee.

After spending a decade in big tech, Olga is deeply familiar with impostor syndrome, burnout, and the struggles to keep up every day. Through her films and media projects, she creates spaces where people are reminded they are not alone.

Scan QR code to learn more, or visit https://www.coffeecupproductions.com/

Where Silence Gets Loud:

Poems on Introspection, Acceptance, and Letting Go

by Olga Gabris

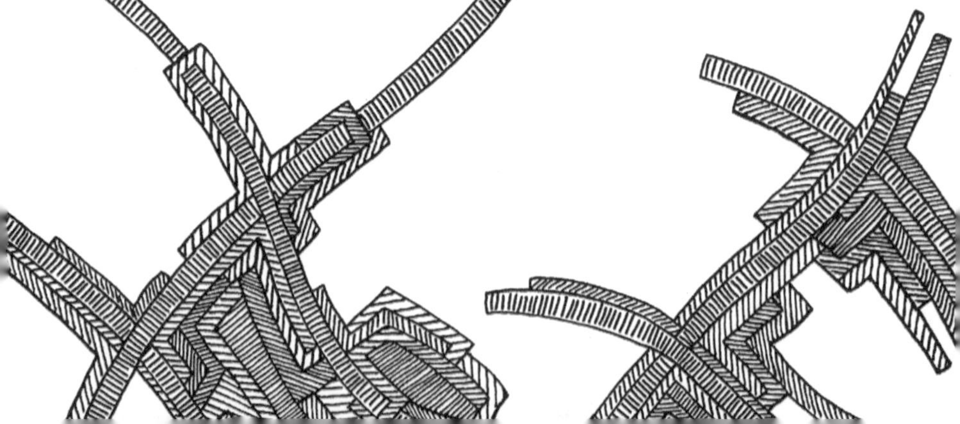

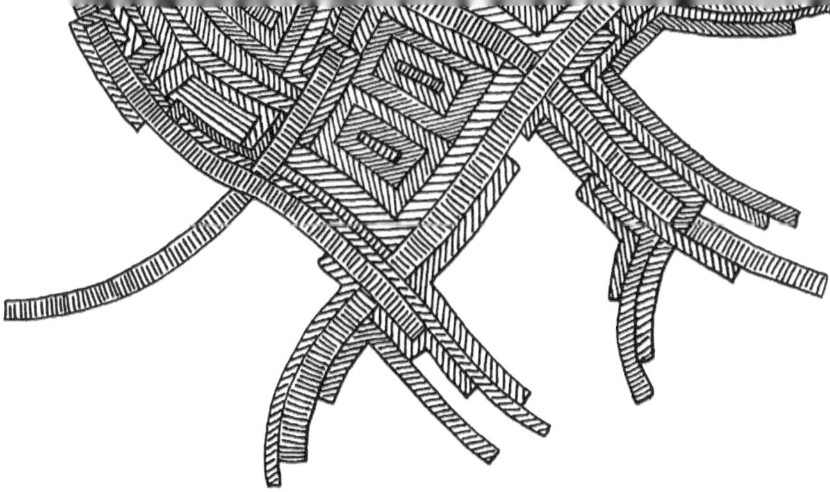

$16.99
ISBN 979-8-9963853-0-0
51699>
9 798996 385300

www.ingramcontent.com/pod-product-compliance
Lightning Source LLC
LaVergne TN
LVHW100318210926
848480LV00003B/1178
* 9 7 9 8 9 9 6 3 8 5 3 0 0 *